Sara DeGraff

How to Dance With Life

How to Dance with Life

Also By Sara DeGraff

Night Time (poetry)

Sara DeGraff

How to Dance With Life
Third Edition

Sara DeGraff

Timeless Avatar Press
New York • **London** • **Vancouver**

How to Dance With Life
© Copyrighted in July 2000
Published in 2000, 2005, 2025 by Timeless Avatar Press
ISBN 0-978-0-9781567-9-4
All rights reserved. No part of this book may be used or reproduced in any manner whatsoever without written permission.

Sara DeGraff

I thank Lenore Stoneberg and Evens Saint Dic for their input and support. I dedicate this book to my family and friends with love.

How to Dance with Life

Sara DeGraff

Table of Contents

Vision	x
Preface	x

Choosing the Dance: Manifestos

Know Thyself	15
Define Yourself	17
Believe In Yourself	18
Take Control of Your Life	20
Take Care of Yourself	22
Believe in Something	23
Take a Stand	27
Dream Big	29

Choosing the Music: Values

Acknowledge Your Roots	28
Respect Your Parents	29
Respect Your Children	30
Respect the Elderly	31
Befriend Yourself	33

How to Dance with Life

Be Committed	34
Strive To Be Honest	36
Strive To Be Kind	38
Be Content with What You Have	41
Never Judge A Book By Its Cover	43

Learning the steps: Techniques

Always Be Prepared for Changes	45
Avoid Traveling the Same Road Twice	47
Be Careful Of What You Ask For	50
Control Your Anger	51
Do Not Hurry Love	53
Do Not Burn Your Steps	55
Do Not Fight Other People's Battles	56
Face Your Opponent	57

Find Your Own Pace	59
Never Be Afraid To Ask For Help	60
Protect Yourself	61
Do Not Humiliate Others	62
Give a Hand	64
Learn From Your Mistakes	66
Practice Humility	68
Clean Up Your Mess	69
Learn To Negotiate	70

Watch Your Steps	71
Learn Detachment	72
Learn To Empathize	73
Learn To Trust	74
Listen to Your Intuitiveness	75
Do Not Postpone	78
Do Not Give Up	79
Never Sell Yourself Short	83
Fear Not	84
Grande finale: Summing up	
Ask for Forgiveness	88
Give Thanks	90
Take Notes	92
Your favorite quotes	93
How do you dance with life?	94

Vision

I see people at
The end of their journey
Cursing at life's broken promises
Advertising frauds
And misleading signposts
I see newborns being welcomed
With symphonies and fanfares Exiting
unnoticed
At the end of their journey.
I see people going to their maker
Exhausted and disappointed at the sum of
their lives' accomplishments.
I see people born inconspicuous
Turning into the greatest teachers of our times and
living forever in our minds.
Are those being welcomed
With symphonies and fanfares
At the beginning of their journey Really
at the end of their glory?

Sara DeGraff

Preface

Find a tuneful life and move to the sound of its music. Fix any of life's broken musical strings, tune them and adapt your steps to the cadence of life. We are all sons and daughters of the Universe and our existence on this earth is not accidental.

We are here for a purpose. It just happens that in order to fulfill our purpose and participate fully in the decision-making process affecting our being, we have to follow rules. How to Dance with Life is a set of guidelines to show you how to achieve this goal. There are times in everybody's life when one has to take inventory and decide what works and what does not.

We should be thankful for having been given the opportunity to take part in such an exciting journey. We are special and intelligent beings. We can make the Dean's List and become honor students. If we don't uphold our good standing in the School of Life, we may delay the accomplishment of our mission on earth.

To be successful in this journey, we need to keep reminding ourselves of how special and lucky we are. We need to keep honoring ourselves. We need to remember that we are part of something big and that we have made it so far because of our uniqueness.

You are sent here by a higher Being and you hold a piece of life's puzzle that only you can put into place. Remember: you have a very important mission and a major responsibility to humankind. You cannot fail. You owe it to others and to yourself to succeed.

Of course, there will be challenges in your path: betrayals, losses and people trying to hold you back. These are not "failures."

These challenges can be used as lessons learned to better your life and achieve your life's purpose. As long as you are aware of your role in this gigantic universe, you are armed and able to handle whatever life brings to you. In order to better enjoy your journey and experience life as you should, divest yourself of any preconceived ideas. When we are born into this world, we go through a process best described by Wordsworth in his "Ode of Intimations of Immortality"

> *Our birth is but a sleep and a forgetting*
> *The soul that rises with us, our life's*
> *Star Hath had elsewhere its setting, and come from afar:*
> *Not in entire forgetfulness,*
> *And not utter nakedness*
> *But trailing clouds of glory do we come*
> *From God, who is our home:*
> *Heaven lies about us in our infancy!*
> *Shades of the prison begin to close Upon the growing boy,*
> *But he beholds the light, and whence it flows,*
> *He sees it in his joy;*
> *The youth, who daily farther from the east*
> *Must travel, still is Nature's priest, Is on his way attended;*
> *At length the man perceives it die away.*

That process depicted by Wordsworth is vital to our soul's growth. To achieve our mission on earth, we need to empty our cup of any preconceived judgment.

Most of us feel lost because we have no memory of the whereabouts of our soul before this journey. Although we may have inkling through a phenomenon called déjà vu that we have been to certain places, that we have met some people and committed some actions before, we cannot be certain.

Sara DeGraff

It is difficult for some of us to discover what our purpose here on earth is because of that very uncertainty. Even when we find out what our mission is, it is sometimes impossible to fulfill it. For as we become older and preoccupied with the hardships of life, we easily lose our way.

We become caught up in the material world and lose touch with our spiritual selves. We forget we have a body and a soul that have to be in tune with one another in order to have a balanced life and a clear path. That is why so many of us find it impossible to reclaim our birthright.

It is not too late for us to find our way; to find the face that we had before the world was made. As William Butler Yeats remarked: "I am looking for the face I had before the world was created."

We are all looking for that. Happily, it is not too late for any one of us to find that face because through whichever world we opt to travel, there are guides to show us the way. Whether physical or spiritual, each world possesses different teachers to test our abilities, and grade us according to how well we apply to our daily lives the lessons we have learned. These guides or teachers give us a "pass", moving us from one level to the next. Or they give us a "fail", making us repeat the same lessons until we learn them. The lessons are along our path in the form of adversities, traps, and pitfalls designed to challenge us and try to keep us from moving toward our destiny and from returning home to our true selves. The traps or pitfalls could be in the form of people trying to hold us back by making us lose faith in ourselves and doubt our ability to complete our task here on earth. This is why we must be strong. This is why we must also regard life as a play in which different roles are given to each of us. The roles of some people in our lives are to teach us, to challenge us, and to create all kinds of delusions to trick us and to make things difficult for us in the School of Life. The higher your level in the School of Life, the more difficult the lessons become. That is why no matter how difficult those actors want to make life appear to be, you will find that it is really simple if you follow life's rules and learn from your experiences.

Try not to panic when things seem difficult; ultimately, things work out.

Sir Francis Bacon told the scholar of life to avoid the stumbling blocks to truth, particularly the "influence of a fragile and unworthy authority".

Remember that you are the master of your destiny and only you have the power to design it. I hope that <u>How to Dance With Life</u> and its principles can help you achieve the life full of joy and happiness that you were born to experience.

Know Thyself

One of the most important principles to a complete life is to know thyself. The knowledge of oneself makes it easy to understand others. It also prepares you to deal with people's shortcomings.

Connect with your higher self to find out who you are. Understand that this inquiry cannot be done in a hurry; it requires spending time with yourself. It also requires enough objectivity to discern what is real from what is false. When you are examining yourself, you are both judge and interested party at the same time.

There is a risk of being unable to be completely impartial or to become acquainted with a part of yourself you do not really like. Despite that risk, you must go for it, for as Socrates puts it: "an unexamined life is not worth living."

A good friend of mine, who is close to retiring from his career, one day, confessed to me that he did not know himself. When I inquired about his reason for not getting to know himself, he replied it was because he had spent all his life going after things, he thought were important --- having a successful career, making ends meet to support his children --- so that he never took time to delve into his inner self. After a moment of silence, he went on explaining that maybe he had not taken the time to go through the process of introspection because he was afraid of meeting a monster.

This man believed that he was not a very nice person. He convinced himself of that fact, to avoid meeting the demons of his existence. We all have to face our demons sometimes and exorcize them. Get to know yourself, no matter how hard it is. Make sure that while doing so you identify the connection between different events, which have occurred at different times in your life, because all of them are interrelated.

Analyze patterns. Whatever happened has its reason. Pay attention to every detail of your life because they are all part of your life's puzzle ready to be put into place. How you reacted to those events when they occurred can help you know yourself better, and help you come to terms with why certain situations worked out better than others.

Knowing yourself can help you improve your weak points and reinforce your strong ones. Do not be one of those people who are always in a hurry and most of the time go in unproductive circles. Aspire to go in ascending spirals. Slow down; take time to admire the beauty of creation. Find a quiet place where you can be alone with nature. Take time to sit under a tree, and, in the quietness of your heart, interrogate your Creator.

Wait for His answer in the silence of your heart while you communicate with yourself, for whatever answer you are seeking is inside of you. I believe that we all came here with a blueprint of our lives deeply imprinted in our souls, buried under the chaotic tracks of our busy existence.

Define Yourself

There are people who go through life projecting more than who they really are and some displaying less. In life, it is important to paint your own picture of yourself, instead of letting others do it for you.

It is important to define yourself through your views, actions and the boundaries you set. No one knows you better than yourself; therefore, do not let others depict you in a manner that you are not.

Speak up before it is too late. I've seen many people's lives ruined because they failed to define themselves. If you do not introduce yourself, others will do it for you. And they may draw a portrait that looks nothing like you.

Believe In Yourself

When you believe in yourself, other people's actions do not affect you as much as they would if you lacked faith in yourself. Others' perceptions of you and their attempts to put holes in your dreams do not matter as long as you remain true to yourself.

Being true, to oneself, means to live a life of harmony and congruity. When you believe in yourself, you are not afraid to dare to experience life.

Remember that each one of us is unique and has talents that no one else has. It is up to us to use our talents to bear fruit; otherwise, they will go to waste.

Use whatever ability you have to create better lives and to educate people. Utilize your talents, cultivate them, and put them at the service of humanity. By sharing your talents with others, they will replicate and perpetuate themselves. By keeping them to yourself, they may be taken away from you, or wither. That is why it is necessary for you to go out and experience life. Do not be scared to take risks. Do not be afraid to open a new door. You never know what may be waiting for you behind it.

Whatever it is, good or bad, you have the power to handle it. Believe in yourself. Do not be afraid of the unknown! It is by facing new challenges that we get to know ourselves and learn to assess our weaknesses and strengths. Those who are afraid of the unknown are not moving forward but standing still.

Open that new door because you do not want to spend the rest of your life wondering what might have become of your life if you had had faith in yourself. Make sure when you do open that door to turn on the light so everyone can admire your creation through the good use of your gifts.

Do not be like the servant mentioned in Matthew 25, entrusted with the one talent, who believed so little in himself that he did not allow his talent to bear fruit. As the Lord entrusted talents to his servants according to their abilities, so is your talent given to you by your Creator according to your ability to make use of it.

If your burden seems too heavy for you to carry, it is because your lack of self-confidence is blocking you from discovering your strengths. Remember that whatever life's challenges are, you are well equipped to wrestle with them. All you have to do is believe in yourself.

Take Control of Your Life

Do not let other people set the tone for how you should live your life. You know better than anyone what your vision of life is, what your dream is and how to make it happen. No matter what people advise you to do, in the end you will be the one to pay for the consequences of your actions. People will be more likely to share in and benefit from your successes than your misfortunes.

No matter how people try to be involved in your life, they are usually spectators. They are just there to test or challenge your aptitude for the School of Life. The script of your life is only written for you. It's in every cell of your being. Only you are the master of your destiny because you have the lead role. Be the master of your destiny by controlling what enters your sacred sanctuary called life. Do not let negative thoughts and negative people invade your space in the Universe.

For years, I had given people power over my life because I wanted to fill a void, a meaningless existence. I let them manipulate and use me because I was afraid that by putting an end to their mischief in my life, I would see them walk out of my life, leaving it empty. I wanted to please others so much that I shortchanged my life.

Now that I think about it, I realize that I also used those people by giving them a false sense of grandeur and security. Those people were as petrified as I was of stepping into the shoes of their destinies. They hid their own fears, insecurities and imperfections behind their misdeeds and manipulations in order to feel in control. They were as afraid as I was to find the face they had before they started their journey on earth.

I was afraid to meet my higher self, the real me. I did not want it to be disappointed in me. As a result, I let other people run my life and I reaped the consequences.

I ask you to take proper dance steps with grace and style conformed to the cadence and the laws of the Universe. Play an active part in your life! Rule it! And as Walt Whitman wrote: "Oh while I live, to be the ruler of life, not a slave, to meet life as a powerful conqueror, and nothing exterior to me shall ever take command of me."

Take Care of Yourself

Treat yourself whenever you can to the best things life has to offer. Pamper yourself. If you do not, nobody else will. Do not be afraid to say: "I love you," to yourself, and to acknowledge life as a precious gift that needs to be cherished. Stand in front of a mirror as often as you can to praise your body, and thank each of its parts for duties or services well performed.

Respect your body; it is your temple, your sanctuary. You owe it to yourself not to contaminate the temple of your life. If it happens for reasons independent of your will, cleanse yourself through prayer and meditation.

After going through the cleansing process, be careful not to put yourself in the same predicament as before. Prayer and meditation should be taken seriously. Do not misuse them.

Take care of your mind by creating a healthy environment and by meditating. Remember your mental and physical selves have to work together in order for you to live a harmonious and enjoyable life.

Believe in Something

Since the beginning of time, there have been many arguments as to why people believe what they believe. Some have died or were killed because of their beliefs. The truth is that those people argued or died because of their fear of being alone in this majestic Universe. They fought because of their need to make sense of their existence, and to give a purpose to it.

We all need to believe in something in order to make sense of our existence. We need to know that our existence is not the result of some kind of accident or coincidence. We need to know that there is a logical explanation for why we are here on earth.

The fact that people believe in something gives them a sense of security, a sense of belonging. A good example of people's sense of security when they believe in something is their belief in God. God, this Supreme Being, this Higher Force (no matter how you refer to Him in your religion) does marvelous things in people's lives. If He did not exist already, we would have to invent Him.

Throughout the history of humankind, there has never been a more positive catalyst for change in the lives of most people. The idea of our actions being guided and watched over by this Higher Being keeps most of us in line. What would you do if everywhere you turned, people misunderstood you, or if your family, friends and lovers turned their backs on you, leaving you to grapple with this Universe? How would you dance with life?

We do not want to be abandoned by Him, and confront this majestic Universe alone. We hold on to Him tightly because we do not want to give up the idea of being under His protection and under the protection of His invisible armies. I ask those of you who believe in God, can you imagine how frightening and empty your life would be without the thought of Him? What would you do when a family member is sick and you feel hopeless because no one can make an accurate diagnosis?

I am a social scientist and I am trained to be objective. Although I have never seen God, I would not trade my belief in Him for any scientific explanation in the world. I need Him in my life, that invisible Father of mine, even when he ignores my cry to Him. I need to be able to commune with Him in the silence of an empty chapel with a lighted candle. I need His comforting words through the lips of a priest, a pastor, a rabbi, a guru, swami or a spiritual master whenever I can listen to them.

I also need the soothing effects of reading the Bible. I have read many books in my lifetime, but I have never read a more inspiring one than the Bible. It contains everything one needs to know in order to live a well-balanced life. It has all the rules of life.

No matter what your beliefs are, keep an open-mind and read the Bible. If you are an atheist, you may read it out of curiosity; you also may have a life-changing experience. I am not imposing my belief in God upon you. What I am doing is encouraging you to believe in something---whatever you may choose --- as long as it helps you make sense of the Universe and empowers you to live a well-balanced life.

When I was younger, I questioned the existence of God every day and even wrote the following about my inquiry:

> *I wake up in the morning*
> *Trying to define what is good?*
> *What is bad?*
> *I wake up in the morning*
> *Trying to please God*

But, who is God?
What does He want from me?
What does He expect from me?
I Wake up in the morning
Looking for guidance
Hoping that one day I will find the truth.

That thirst for the truth led me to explore a wealth of literature related to God and made me attend all types of Churches regardless of their denomination. I questioned what they called God in their search for answers. As I grew older, instead of questioning His existence, I affirmed His existence in my cry for help:

God, I know that you exist
But every time I try to get close to you
Something always comes between us. God,
do not hide your face from me
Because you are the rock that
I attach myself to when I am afraid of falling.
God, you are my weapon against fear
You are my hope that tomorrow will be better

As I matured, I wanted to tell everyone how good God has been to me, and how He has never failed me. I wanted to release my fear of testifying to God's glory and compassion. I wanted to acknowledge my relationship with God in front of multitudes:

I want to give Him praise and thanks.
I want to tell you how
He lifted me up out of a deep hole.
I want to tell you how
He gave me a bath of purification.
And washed away all my transgressions.
I want to tell you how
He chased away.

Sara DeGraff

All the darkness that was around me.
By surrounding me with a shiny bright light
That lightened and guided my steps.

God has done a lot for me. He has been my anchor throughout my life. I chose to hold on to him, although I have been exposed to many other visions of God. I have received spiritual blessings through Buddhist chants, and Hindu prayers. I have felt the deep sense of the Creator's presence through the African drum and the Salish drum. When I admire the beauty of the creation of Universe, everything is so well organized that I cannot imagine my being here as the result of an accident. To me there is a Creator and that Creator is God.

Take a Stand

Stand by your beliefs. I have seen people going through life drifting from right to left because they are afraid to stand up and speak out. Be ready to be blackballed because not all stands are popular ones. Some stands require going against powerful forces and may even endanger the lives of your loved ones.

Other positions are harmless and more popular. However, no matter what your stand is, it requires courage and determination to persevere. As Gandhi stated: *"The Golden rule is to act fearlessly upon what one believes to be right."*

It is important to take a stand for it is heartless to go through life seeing injustice being done to people and to be in a position to denounce those actions and to not do something about it. It is cruel to go through life with the attitude of see no evil and hear no evil.

You have a responsibility to do something when you see people in inhumane predicaments, because their lives may very well depend on your speaking out. No matter how difficult things become, do not abandon your choice. I have seen people devastated by actions committed by people who failed to stand by their resolutions.

I have seen hypocrites pretending to stand for causes as long as those causes conveniently served their own purposes, and who then walk away from their leaders, loved ones, friends during the greatest battles of their lives. Those hypocrites are individuals who go wherever the wind of opportunity blows. They are the weak links in every organization, association or party. Do not be one of those people.

Stand firm for what you believe; stand by your resolutions no matter what. For as Martin Luther King said:

"The ultimate measure of a man is not where he stands in moments of comfort and convenience but where he stands at a time of challenge and controversy."

Dream Big

Dream and think big because there is really no limit to what one can achieve. We are the ones who set our own limits in our minds. We are the ones who bargain with life and take what we think we deserve. As James Allen said: *"Dream lofty dreams, and as you dream you shall become. Your vision is really the promise of what you shall one day be. Your idea is the prophecy of what you shall at last unveil."*
I know what some of you are thinking right now, that you have dreamed big all your life and that it never got you anywhere. Now stop and take time to examine yourself to find out how much you wanted to fulfill your dreams.
Stop now and ask yourself whether or not you had worked hard enough and given your dreams your best shot.

Dreaming big is not enough; you must also take steps toward fulfilling your dreams. You must visualize whatever you want to achieve by having a clear picture in your mind and release it to the Universe for manifestation.
As Henry David Thoreau advised:

> *If one advances confidently in the direction of his dreams and endeavors to live the life which he has imagined, he will meet with a success unexpected in common hours. He will put some things behind, will pass an invisible boundary; new, universal; and more liberal laws will begin to establish themselves around and within him; or old laws will be expanded and interpreted in his favor in a more liberal sense and he will live with license of a higher order of beings.*

Acknowledge Your Roots

Never forget where you came from, no matter how humble your roots may be. If you do, you will be forfeiting a good part of yourself, which is essential to move toward your destiny. Your roots are your foundation. Without clear acknowledgment of your roots, you are like fallen leaves blown by the wind ceaselessly.

How can you find out who you are and where you want to go if you deny your roots? Your roots unquestionably contain valuable information about what makes you who you are today.

Acknowledging your roots does not mean that you have to let whatever missteps you took in the past hold you back. It means embracing the essence of who you truly are, and making sure that the necessary ingredients needed for your journey are where they should be. Your "self" is made of many different pieces, from many different periods of your journey.

Respect Your Parents

The first time you opened your eyes, the people there to welcome you were your parents. As a matter of fact, they were entrusted with your well-being even before you were born. For months, you heard voices and in a dark place you tried to make sense of what was going on. Although you could feel the love contained in some of the voices you were hearing, you still wanted to be reassured.

Your mother suffered a great ordeal to take you out of the dark tunnel of her womb to make you see the light. The first time you opened your eyes, there were your parents smiling; hugging you and making you feel safe.

When you took your first step, they were there to hold your hands. They were patient and surrounded you with love when you crawled and fell countless times until you could stand up. They accompanied you throughout your journey until you could fly on your own. Even after they left this world, their spirits never left you.

There are people who swear that they have felt their departed parents still guiding them, and loving them. This is how strong your bond is with your parents.

Honor your parents, even when they make mistakes. Do not expect them to be supermen or superwomen, but just regular people with an almost impossible task.

Respect Your Children

Parents, respect your children! Honor your commitment, for they did not ask to be born. You had the means at your fingertips to prevent yourself from becoming parents, and you took that responsibility. Do not make them pay for your choice because they had no say in it.

You became entrusted with their guardianship by accepting to become parents; you have pledged to lend them your eyes so they could see through them at the beginning of their journey. You have accepted the responsibility of becoming their first teachers in their first classrooms of their lives.

You have the most important roles in their lives because if you do not live up to your responsibility as their teachers and teach them well, they may be physically and mentally handicapped for the rest of their lives. Do not use them for your own purposes.

Take care of your children and love them as much as you would like to be loved and cared for. At the end of your journey, the role is going to be reversed; your children will, then, become your guardians.

They will have to put their senses at your disposal in order for you to continue your journey. Just as you held your children's hands so they could take their first steps and stand up, they will also hold your hands when your feet are too tired from having taken too many steps or when you have stood too long.

Respect the Elderly

When children are born, they are like the sunrise because they are at the beginning of their journey. They are beautiful to look at. Their innocence is like sunshine spreading its wings over the universe.

When people get old, sometimes they are regarded as unimportant beings whose era has passed and who now have to step aside to give way to the newcomers: their children. We often hear the saying that "children are our future." Children are our future in the sense that they have to help carry the torch of life forward, and continue where the elders left off; but that does not make children more important than elders.

Children and elders are just part of the process of change and renewal of life as the Universe goes on. As said in the Bible, "Rebuke not an elder, but entreat him as a father, the elder women as mothers." In the past, before people lost their moral compass, being a father or a mother meant a lot.

Unfortunately, it does not mean much these days. I have seen people treat their parents as no more than a ticket for a better meal. I have seen elders being robbed of everything they worked for in their younger years, by their children who were supposed to take care of them.

I have witnessed their homes being sold right from under their nose by their lazy children because of the effects of old age. I have seen many promises being broken to them by their children who want to claim their inheritance before its due time. I have seen so many heartbreaking injustices being done to our elders because people fail to realize that there is beauty in a sunset as well as in a sunrise.

Elders are just like the sunset at the end of the day. They have already gone through the steps that children who are at the beginning of their journey are about to take. Elders, because they have already gone through the day are a wealth of wisdom and knowledge. They can help guide the steps of the young ones.

Amadou Hampaté Ba, a great writer and defender of African tradition from Mali once said: *"tout vieillard qui meurt en Afrique est une bibliotèque qui brûle,"* that is, *"The death of an elder is similar to a burned down library."*

In Africa, elders are treated with utmost respect and the younger generations turn to them for guidance. In some countries of the Caribbean and Africa, elders inculcate through story telling moral values to the younger generations. The elders of the aboriginal tribes in Canada's prairies live and teach the Eternal Return: nothing is ever lost forever and every misfortune will transform to fortune for some being in the unending chain of generations.

Please honor the elders; celebrate their journey on earth. They are just as valuable to the Universe as the children are. If you ever have any doubt, wake up early one day to admire the beauty of the sunrise and then take the time to witness the soothing effect of a sunset in a late afternoon.

You will deduce for yourself how they both complement one another and that there is beauty in sunset as well as in sunrise. Always keep in mind that each ending is a beginning and each beginning is an ending: never-ending renewal.

Befriend Yourself

Develop a relationship with yourself based upon trust and respect. Reward yourself when you do things of which you are proud and reprimand yourself when you commit actions of which you are not so proud. Make promises to yourself and keep them.

Do not betray yourself to please others!

When you give too much to people you may create greed and when you give too little, you may create resentment. Know that you will never be able to please everyone you meet.

The first person you should pay attention to is yourself; not in a selfish manner but in a way that brings congruity to your actions, and harmony into your life.

Throughout my life, I befriended many people and animals. Some of those beings brought me joy; others caused me great grief. They stayed in my life for just enough time to fulfill their purposes.

But whether I like it or not, I am stuck with myself for the duration of my life. Just as I am stuck with myself, so are you with yourself. Therefore, it is in your best interest to befriend yourself for you will never have a better friend than yourself.

No matter what, accept yourself with all your virtues and imperfections. Be so in tune with yourself that no storm can shake your foundation. And as the saying goes: "Befriend yourself and you will never be alone."

Be Committed

Whatever you do, give it one hundred percent without hesitation. Hesitation makes you waste valuable time. I am not advising you to act carelessly without thinking, for you must always weigh the pros and the cons of your actions. What I am advising you to do is to take actions after thinking things through thoroughly.

Try not to do anything halfway, otherwise you will only obtain half results and get halfway to achieving your goal. Whatever you are doing, do it fully. Love fully, feel fully and live fully.

If you are not committed to what you are doing, you will never achieve anything. And by not achieving anything you will go through life with a sense of low self-worth, especially if you compare yourself to others who have managed to make it in the world.

Success is not a matter of chance, but a matter of choice and only you have the power to make that choice.

Being committed to whatever you are doing is one sure way to achieve success because it allows you to keep your eyes on the prize no matter how difficult your journey becomes. As Goethe wrote:

> *Until one is committed there is hesitancy, the chance to draw back, always ineffectiveness. Concerning all acts of initiative and creation.... There is one elementary truth... ignorance... kills countless ideas and splendid plans...that the moment one definitely commits oneself, then providence moves ... All sort of things occur to help one that would never otherwise have occurred... A whole of stream of events issues from the decision; raising in one's favor All unforeseen incidents and meetings and material assistance which no one could have dreamed would have come this way...*

Whatever you can do or dream, you can begin it...Boldness has genius, power and magic in it...Begin it now.

Strive To Be Honest

Try to be as honest as you can be. Some people have a tendency to use dishonesty to avoid confrontation, retaliation and discovery.

Others practice dishonesty to obtain things they would not have gotten if they were to be honest. And there are others who do it to protect themselves and their privacy. It does not matter why other people choose to be dishonest.

When you have to make a decision between lying and telling the truth, always put people first, by weighting whether or not your lies will impact their lives adversely.

Try not to do to others what you would not want them to do to you. As a Muslim mystic named Al Ghazali stated: *"If you want to know the foulness of lying for yourself, consider the lying of someone else and how you shun it and despise the man and regard his communication as foul."*

The 19th Century German Philosopher, Immanuel Kant wrote: *"By a lie, a man throws away and, as it were, annihilates his dignity as a man."*

Being honest is without a doubt a difficult undertaking since we live in an era in society where telling the truth takes backstage to back stabbing.

The truth is now known as the version of the truth. That version of the truth can appear to be more truthful than the truth itself, depending on how eloquent is the person telling it, and how big is his wallet.

The bigger your wallet is, the more powerful you are, the more weight your version has and the more convincing it is. It is up to you, to know which rules you want to follow: The rules of the dysfunctional society we live in or the laws of the Universe where whatever evil you do always comes back to haunt you. Nevertheless, I urge you at least to give honesty a try. As stated in Philippians 4:8:

> *Whatsoever things are true, whatsoever things are honest, whatsoever things are just, whatsoever things are pure, whatsoever things are lovely, whatsoever things are of good report; if there is any virtue, and there be any praise, think on these things.*

Strive To Be Kind

Be kind to others and strive to do the right thing against all odds. It is the only way to be at peace with yourself.

Whenever you are tempted to hurt or harm someone, pause for a moment and ask yourself: "How would I feel if someone else were doing the same thing to me?" If the answer is "I would not feel very good," then do not proceed. When you do something good and kind it is like depositing money into your account in the bank of life and then when you do something bad and unkind, you run an overdraft on that account.

Don't you have better things to do with your life than to create bad debts that will surely mess up your account in the School of Life? Remember: "We reap what we sow." As Socrates so astutely remarked:

> *The wicked man is never truly happy even when stuffing himself with food, even when enjoying his riches to the utmost. One who lives by oppressing others can never feel the true happiness of a virtuous man. One who lives righteously is happy even when he undergoes poverty, suffering and death.*

Be Content with What You Have

Be grateful for what you have and do not envy those who appear to have more than you do. Because, somewhere in the world, there are people who have less and who would be happy to be in your shoes. As long as you can eat, drink fresh water, have a bed to sleep in and a roof over your head, count your blessings.

In life, not all beings have the same gifts, abilities and aptitudes to take advantage of opportunities presented to them.

Not all people have the same quest. Different quests require different life tools, different dance steps, and different capacities and velocities according to the time allotted to complete these missions.

Each quest requires specific skills. We also have different lessons to learn from life. That is why some have more material goods than others, or are happier than others. All you can do is try to go after the things you want out of life and follow to the best of your abilities the laws of the Universe. Then let go and let God.

As the poet Douglas Malloch says:
> *If you can't be a pine on top of the hill,*
> *Be a scrub in the valley- but be*
> *The best little scrub by the side of the hill;*
> *Be a bush, if you can't be a tree.*
> *If you can't be a bush, be a bit of the grass,*
> *And some highway happier make;*
> *If you can't be a Muskie,*
> *then just be a bass*
> *But the liveliest bass in the lake!*
> *We can't be all captains,*

> *We've got to be crew*
> *There's something for all of us here.*
> *There's big work to do and there's lesser*
> *To do and the task*
> *We must do is near*
> *If you can't be*
> *A highway then just be*
> *A trail*
> *If you can't be the sun,*
> *Be a star.*
> *It isn't by size that you win or you fail*
> *Be the best of whatever you are.*

If you understand life as did Malloch, you will not waste time envying others.

As Thomas Moore cautioned: "*Envy can be consuming. It can crowd out every other thought and emotion with its pungency. It can make a person distracted, 'touched' as we say, aching for life, position, and possessions of others.*" My neighbors have happiness, money, success, children --- why don't I? My friend has a good job, looks, luck --- what's wrong with me?

There might be a good dose of self-pity in envy, but it's the longing that is so bitter. Envy eats at the heart. If you want to be happy, learn to be content with what you have. Material possessions do not buy peace of mind nor do they buy longevity, nor do they spare you from pain and disappointment.

What good is life if one spends one's whole journey worrying about things that will not matter at the end of one's journey?

Never Judge A Book By Its Cover

Never accept anyone or anything at face value. Know that no matter what is visible, there is always more. Usually what is seen is only the tip of the iceberg. To discover more requires digging deeper. You see the whole picture by paying attention to details. To discover what is beyond the surface requires patience and understanding.

You have to be willing to accept people for who they are. No matter how perfect you think people may appear, that is usually an illusion.

Do not judge people before you have a chance to really get to know them and discover all the facts about them. No matter how awful their actions may appear to be, take time to think about yourself and all the foolish things you have done throughout your journey; as it is stated in Titus 3:3: *"For we ourselves also were sometimes foolish, disobedient, deceived, serving divers lusts and pleasures living in malice and envy, hateful and hating one another."*

Do not judge a book by its cover because things and people are not always what they appear to be. For example, you may have a student who comes every morning to school without having done his homework. As a teacher, you may be inclined to send him home and stigmatize him for not being a dedicated student. On the surface it may appear so, but in reality, he may be a smart student lacking guidance.

I have met a lot of people in my lifetime who at first glance appeared to be spiteful but who turned out to be caring people. Deep within themselves they were really good people crying for help. All it takes sometimes is a little kindness and understanding to turn them into the most wonderful beings, living up to their full potential.

Do not judge a book by its cover until you can read all its pages and fully understand the contents; people usually project only what they want you to see.

There are so many stereotypes in our society that we sometimes lose sight of what is real and what is not.

Always Be Prepared for Changes

Do what you must do to survive. Plan as much as you can, and leave as little to chance as you can. Come up with all the possible strategies to avoid drowning in the sea of life.

Chances are, if you are old enough to read these guidelines, you have traveled through your journey far enough to know that things do not always work out as planned.

To be conscious of that fact allows you to be able to adjust quickly to both new situations, and new guidelines in the School of Life, both of which are necessary for you to properly adjust your dance steps to the rhythm of the Universe.

One night, as I lay in my bed, taking inventory of the day that had just passed; I gazed out my window from my fifth-floor apartment in Kew Gardens Hills. I caught a glimpse of the most beautiful moon that I had ever seen. It was so amazing that I decided to turn off the light to better admire this magnificent creation of God: in the dark, and in the tranquility of my room, my sanctuary.

Because the full moon's beauty mesmerized me, I persuaded myself that I was going to spend the rest of the night contemplating it while meditating. Little did I know that the clouds were going to cover it and deprive me of its comforting presence. Soon after, rain gently knocked against my window. I fell asleep thinking about the fleeting aspects of life.

In life there is no permanency, rather it is here today, gone tomorrow!

When the full moon gave way to the clouds, that night, I became unhappy because I was not prepared for the changes in the sky. I made myself comfortable to enjoy a night gazing at a full moon that only lasted a few hours. I was not ready for it to disappear so soon.

No matter how good things are, you ought to be prepared for the unexpected. Being ready for the unexpected does not mean that you should expect a negative outcome in everything you do or that you should only wish upon a star. It means that you should be awake to the fact as stated in Ecclesiastes Chapter Three:

> *To everything there is a season and a time to every purpose under the sun:*
> *A time to be born, and a time to die;*
> *A time to keep and a time to cast away*
> *A time to plant and a time to pluck up that which is planted:*
> *A time to kill, a time to heal,*
> *A time to break down and a time to build up;*
> *A time to weep and a time to laugh*
> *A time to laugh and a time to dance;*
> *A time to cast away stones and a time to gather stones;*
> *A time to embrace and a time to refrain from embracing,*
> *A time to get and a time to lose;*
> *A time to keep, and a time to cast away*
> *A time to rend and a time to sew;*
> *A time to keep silent and a time to speak out;*
> *A time to love and a time to hate*
> *A time of war and a time of peace*

I could not agree more with this quote because it helps us understand the duality of life and makes us realize how little control we have over matters in this life.

Most of the events that happen in our lives are unexpected and thus we need to be vigilant and prepare for rainy seasons during dry seasons.

Avoid Traveling the Same Road Twice

If you find yourself traveling the same road, it may be because you are going backward or in a circle instead of forward. If that happens, it means that you are not applying yourself in the School of Life and you are being forced to go down the same path.

Slow down and pause before you take another step. Make sure you apply yourself this time. The only way to go is forward and to do so, you need to forget about whatever missteps you have taken in the past. If you can't do that, everything you have gone through, you have gone through in vain.

Do you want to have suffered so many things in vain?
I know a few things about moving forward because this is one of the lessons of life, I've had to repeat several times. I finally understood this lesson after it was made clear to me in one of my dreams.

> *First, in that dream, I was shown a white car on top of a Baptist Church, a church to which I occasionally went when I was a little girl. Second, at one level above the church, ---not immediately on top of the church, but from a distance close enough to the church that I could see both the car, and two of my family members--- there was my late brother Marc who died in 1990 and my older sister having a conversation.*
> *At two levels higher than the car, and one level higher than my family members, I saw myself standing and watching them. I was close enough that I could see both the car and them. I was on a dirt road watching them. Suddenly I saw three men passing by and decided to follow them. They disappeared and tell in my dream-state*
> *I could not tell where they had gone. All I remember*

is that after they disappeared, I found myself at the bottom of a mountain; then I started climbing. When I had reached the middle of the mountain, I was instructed not to look back, to keep climbing. It was very difficult since I was climbing the mountain with my bare hands, and was trying to hold on to whatever I could grab in order not to fall. I do not remember looking back but as I was climbing, I could sense that if I fell, I would land in a deep hole. As instructed in my dream, I kept going until I reached the top. I remember thinking when I got to the top how lonely and peaceful it was, for only a few people had reached the peak. I also remember wondering how I would be able to go back down if I decided to return; then I woke up

I interpret the white car as a material possession and family members as loved ones or people that I had to leave behind in order to move toward my destiny. I share this dream with you as an inspiration to move forward and keep going no matter what.

Remember that life is a journey with many landscapes to explore. As in any journey, you have to travel many roads and leave many travelers behind. As a friend used to say: "many may get in the bus with you but before you get to your destination, most of them will get off."

The people who get on the bus with you may be loved ones, friends, guides or teachers. Not all of us travel to the same distance. Not all of us travel the same path for long. Sometimes you travel only part of the way with someone; either you or he changes planes, buses or trains on the way, or even decides to walk, depending on the duration of the journey or the distance.

To concentrate on your journey, you must keep in mind that any journey has a beginning and an end, an origin and a destination, and a purpose. The only way to get to your destination is to move forward from point A to point B. The purpose of this journey on earth is to learn and grow spiritually. Since it is necessary to explore life's journey thoroughly in order to learn well its lessons you do not want to miss anything that may be critical for achieving your success. By doing so, whatever steps you take while moving toward your destiny will be satisfactory and confident ones.

Be Careful of What You Ask For

Be careful of what you ask for when you pray, especially if you are asking God to bring changes into your life. Be sure you can handle the changes or the things you ask for because you might get them before you know it.

One time I was lost, so lost that I was not sure whether or not I was going to find my way back. I prayed to God to change my life and He did. He did it so quickly that I was not ready for it. I tried to hold on to my predicament because I was afraid of the unknown. But God had other plans for me.

Next time you pray, ask God to guide you in your decisions and choices.

Accept the outcome and have faith that God will guide you and help you obtain the tools that you need to complete your journey on earth.

Control Your Anger

Anger is the most destructive of all negative feelings. There are times we burst out angrily because our sense of worth and self-esteem have been destroyed. We feel betrayed, hurt and wronged by the people we love.

When the thought of this 'affront' haunts us, it causes us to become infuriated and react violently toward the object of our anger. Sometimes we cannot calm down until we make the people who angered us pay for what they did to us. If, for any reason the people or the person who hurt us is not available, then sometimes we project our anger onto people who have nothing to do with the situations that produced our hurt feelings.

By doing so, we find temporary appeasement, but the problem still remains; it is best to honestly face your anger instead of looking for scapegoats. I am not saying that you do not have the right to be angry. Most anger is legitimate because there are more than enough people in society who take pleasure in hurting others for reasons only known to themselves.

The manner in which you express your anger can make all the difference in your life. Before you get enraged, take a moment to ask yourself: who is your anger benefiting, you or the other party? Who is your anger hurting, you or the other party?

Your anger is benefiting the other party because anger clouds your judgment and makes you act in ways detrimental to your mental and physical health. For your sake, you need to take a systematic approach in dealing with that emotion by admitting your anger, identifying its sources and forgiving the persons associated with it. It is feasible to take your life back by re-assuming control of the power over your existence given to unworthy people.

Only time and a strong will can allow you to reclaim your life and release your anger.

Remember when people hurt you, do not get angry; instead look at them with forgiveness in your heart.

Forgiveness does not occur overnight. It is an ongoing process. It requires courage and wisdom from the people who have been wronged. But, take it from someone who has been betrayed and wronged time and again by her friends, lovers and family members, it is possible to forgive.

Do Not Hurry Love

Love takes time. It requires nurturing to gain strength and endurance. Do not rush love! Before you open your heart to love, before you welcome any stranger at the door of your heart, make sure that he/she is not a bushwhack plotting to hurt your feelings.

No matter how captivated you are by someone's physical appearance or charm when you two first meet, do not rush. Attraction does not guarantee a long-lasting relationship or friendship.

I say friendship because I believe that two people who are engaged in any kind of intimacy should be friends, close friends. Unfortunately, we are living in a dysfunctional world where our moral values are in disarray and some people do not care about the feelings of others. Those people will stop at nothing to get what they want.

What they want perhaps are many things. Some are looking for sexual gratification and just want to use their mate to satisfy that need. There are others who are after financial security and prey on people's desires to be loved to get what they want.

Although love is the most powerful force in the Universe, it is definitely not very easy to recognize and we do not usually give it a chance to blossom. Our notion of love is all too often clouded by how it is portrayed in the movies, on television or in novels.

Love, the most powerful feeling that has ever existed, is a very serious undertaking. No one should set sail in the sea of love without preparation; otherwise, one runs the risk of capsizing.

Always take time to get to know your partner and find out the motive behind his or her interest before you become intimate. Always make sure that you both want the same things from life, and share the same views about important issues affecting your everyday lives. Test each other's tolerance toward one another when faced with life's vicissitudes.

It is effortless to be around people when things are going well in their lives: when they are happy, healthy and financially secure. But it takes a lot of understanding and caring to stay around when things are bad. Knowing how your partner is likely to behave in certain situations is crucial to the foundation of any lasting union.

When you give your initial attraction time to manifest itself and you decide to let it blossom, then you can experience the feeling that has inspired the greatest artists, poets, writers and composers throughout the history of humankind.

Do not hurry love because your time will come. We all have another half of us somewhere yearning to reunite with his/her other half. It just takes time to identify him or her because that other half may be in the form of a raw diamond. Your other half may be covered with dust from having traveled the Universe searching for you in order to become whole again. Your significant other may be damaged by all the hard knocks encountered along his or her path and be in need of repair. She or he may be disguised, wearing many hats in order to better carry the other half of the treasure that is guaranteed to produce sparks when made whole again.

Do not hurry love; take time to find it. Do not let yourself be robbed of that precious gift from God. Real love is there for you to experience. When its wind blows your way, it will energize you and it will give you wings. You will never be alone again, even when your soul mate is miles away. You will be strengthened because you will never have to fight any more battles on your own.

Do Not Burn Your Steps

In life, you cannot burn your steps. You always have to put one foot after the other and proceed step by step, that is the only way to arrive at your final destination with the fewest scars and wounds. When you try to burn your steps, you lose the mental and physical strength needed to get to your destination.

Beware of shortcuts because they often prove to be circuitous roads: the types of roads that only offer temporary relief to people trying to escape their pain. In life, there is no shortcut because for every action, there is a reaction. There is no free lunch because there is a price to pay for everything you get from life.

Life has rules to follow. Show me someone who has taken a shortcut, and I will show you someone who is going in an unproductive circle, not an ascending spiral. Be careful not to be one of those people who wastes her life and tries unsuccessfully to escape the lessons of life.

How can you escape life lessons when one of life's rules is not to reveal where the classroom is going to be and who the teacher is? Life's classrooms are unlimited and unexpected, and teachers come in all shapes and forms. The only way to succeed in the School of Life is to be open to being taught at any given moment by anyone or anything

Do Not Fight Other People's Battles

No matter how much you believe in someone's cause, avoid fighting that cause for that person. It is okay to help when you are asked to do so. But never let yourself be so involved in her or his fight that you behave as if it were your fight. By doing so, you put yourself into a vulnerable position.

You may get hurt because the other person may lack the inner fire that you have to win her cause. Because of that lack, you may appear to be too pushy. Her enemies may end up hating you because they may identify you as a threat. They may realize that they would have gotten away with their unjust acts, if it were not for you.

You may end up being the target. It is understandable that people who have suffered from injustices will fight with every cell in their being. But when the person standing next to the target is hurt more than the target person, or feels the pain of that hurt or injustice more than the person being hurt or wronged, then there is a problem.

To right the wrongs that have been done, you will need the consent and the committed participation of the person wronged. If the latter does not realize how cruel the crime committed against her was, no matter how hard you fight for justice, you will end up flat on your face.

Do not fight other people's battles for them because you have enough of a burden to carry yourself, and too many of your own fights to fight in order to get to your destination.

Face Your Opponent

When you are unfairly attacked no matter how frightened you are, stand up and stare your opponent in the eyes and battle until your last breath. Otherwise, what is the use of retaliating if, at every difficult encounter, you are ready to give up.

Some people, when attacked by a worthy opponent, prefer to stay down as long as it takes in order to gather strength and energy before retaliating; others prefer to use other battle tactics. Remember how you choose to retaliate can make a difference between life and death. Try not to endanger yourself while fighting. Fight intelligently. Do not use any weapon that will prevent you from getting to your chosen path.

Know that the reason that your opponent is attacking you is because he wants your downfall. Although not all battles are worth fighting, when an opponent is trying to destroy the very essence of who you are, rob you of your dignity and the fruits of your hard labor, conspiring to destroy everything you have worked for and eradicate you from the face of the earth, you must fight. If you don't defend your life with every cell of your body, all the sacrifices that you made working toward your dreams will go to ashes. Do you remember how many nights you stayed awake working on your dreams? How many people deserted you due to their lack of faith in you? How many times you have fallen and gotten up because you refused to quit? Think how close you are to reaching your goal, to obtaining the rewards of your hard work. You did not get that far in your life to let others ruin it now. You did not get that far by being weak.

Do you remember how much you had to endure and overcome? Or how many tumultuous rivers you had to cross before getting to this point? You were living a decent life trying to make ends meet and minding your own business. You had a dream that you were trying to make come true. Your opponents decided that you had to be stopped because you had bigger dreams than theirs; that you had to be ruined because you refused to play it their way. Do not stop fighting until you overtake them because your life and well-being depend on it.

The weapon used against them will determine either failure or victory; so, choose your weapon well.

When I am unfairly attacked, I usually visualize myself as bright light, and my enemy as darkness and I also use this affirmation:

> *I am not afraid of you are darkness*
> *Therefore, I will overcome you*
> *I will illumine the dark areas*
> *Of your being and your life*
> *I will enter in the most remote places*
> *In your life where no one and probably*
> *not even you have gone before*
> *I am light and you are darkness*
> *And I will not rest*
> *Until I transform you into light.*

You will be aware that your opponents are not only people and things or forces of nature. They may also be forces of thought, of philosophy, or simply of Kant. I will give you a thought which Jean-Paul Sartre used in opposition to the status quo of colonialism in 1963, in the preface to Frantz Fanon's <u>Wretched of the Earth</u>: "we only become what we are by radical and deep-seated refusal of that which others have made of us".

Much of your success in facing your opponent will depend on your success in defining your opponent, and in defining what is in you that puts you in opposition to your opponent.

Find Your Own Pace

Find your own melody and create your own steps to the rhythm of the Universe. Learn your melody well and remember that the rhythms of others should not deter you from accomplishing your goals because the Universe welcomes diversity.

Look at the diversified world we live in with different races, cultures, and religions; in the end, all the melodies become one because we all come from one source and we are all here fulfilling a purpose. As long as those steps are accomplished with grace and dignity and they are not against the laws of the Universe, glide on to the dance floor of life and show your stuff.

Each of us has her own choreography because each of us has her own melody. For different melodies, there are different rhythms. How fast or slow our melody is, depends upon your ability to master the dance steps of life or the laws of the Universe which will, in turn, determine how soon you can follow the steps of your destiny and start fulfilling it.

The length of your melody depends upon how much time is required for you to complete your mission on earth. Therefore, do not worry if the steps of the person next to you do not match yours, just dance to your own melody.

Never Be Afraid To Ask For Help

Do not be ashamed to admit that you do not know how to do something. Do not be embarrassed to ask for help. No human being knows it all. It is in the daily occurrences of life that we learn. There is no shame in asking for help.

Asking for help is sometimes a give and take situation: you are receiving help while you are giving help. You are giving the helping hand a chance to use her talent and to display her knowledge.

The helping hand can find out a lot about herself and discover abilities that she never thought she had. New horizons may open for the helping hand because the person assisted may provide her with food for thought that allows her to put her life's puzzles together. Remember, in life, we reap what we sow.

Do not be afraid to ask for help when it is necessary. It is foolish to go through life alone trying to do things that you do not know how to do when there are people around who can help you. Everyone goes through the same process. And those who make it are the people who were not afraid to ask questions of their parents, teachers and bosses.

There is no problem in asking for help when help is really needed. The problem resides in being lazy and in making people do things that you are capable of doing yourself. If you are afraid to ask for help, then you may never find your way.

Protect Yourself

Protect yourself in any way you can, mentally, physically and legally. Protect yourself mentally by not letting trespassers invade your thoughts.

Protect yourself legally because if you do not, people can take away everything that you have worked for. Commit your every business transaction to paper, by signing a contract. Even when you are associating with family members, a lover or friends, protect yourself.

Make a will; get inventions patented. Try to be as straight as you can be. Be private. Do not broadcast your problems and difficulties. Try to resolve them at home with the people you love in order to protect yourself, because there are many people who do not have your best interests at heart and would not stop at anything to hurt you by using information about you, to impede your advancement.

Protect yourself by keeping abreast of what is going on in your physical, social and emotional environment. Inform yourself about what is going on in the world by reading at least one newspaper per day that can affect your life either positively or negatively.

It is up to you to control the use of that information and protect yourself by getting into any venture with your eyes wide open.

Do Not Humiliate Others

There are people who take pleasure in humiliating others in order to hide their own low sense of worth. There are people who abuse their power and deprive others of their most basic rights. There are still cultures where women do not have a voice.

There are still people humiliating others based on their skin color and their religion. If you fit in any of these categories, stop right now! Stop bigotry! Stop discrimination! Stop anti-Semitism! Stop discriminating against your brothers and sisters no matter how different they are from you. Believe it or not, you are part of the same race: humankind. Without each other, we will not make it on this earth. It is either we all work together or we all perish.

We need each other to face the many challenges of the Universe. Let us unite before it is too late. We all carry a piece of life's puzzle. As small as the piece or as insignificant as it may appear to be, it may be the one piece that helps resolve the major enigma of life.

All pieces have to be put together in order to make the world a better place, not only for our sake but also for generations to come. For that reason, let's not humiliate each other. Bringing shame on others only delays our evolutionary process.

The psychologist, Alfred Adler stated, *"It is the individual who is not interested in his fellow men who has the greatest difficulties in life and provides the greatest injury to others. It is from among such individuals that all human failures spring."*

Instead of degrading others, become interested in them and learn from them, learn about their differences. In these differences may lie certain answers or tools you are looking for to better your journey on earth. See everyone you meet as a new island to discover. Although all islands may be surrounded by water and have trees, you may have one awesome tree where you may feel it is safer to take shelter than others. In one particular island you may be able to find that sense of belonging, security or safety that you never dreamt possible.

See every human being as a new country to visit!

Traveling has taught me that no matter how much research I've done about a country before going there, something was always overlooked. Until you get there you cannot grasp everything there is to know about a place and anticipate what might capture your very being.

Before I went to Egypt, I always thought that nothing I could ever see over there could capture my heart as much as the pyramids. I visited the Pyramids of Giza, the City of the Dead, and the Sphinx, but nothing ever touched me more than seeing one little girl. She was standing at the entrance of the pyramids of Giza begging for money in her little blue dress and white scarf over her head. When I saw her, I felt as if she were my daughter. I felt I was letting her down because I did not adopt her and take her back with me. All kinds of maternal emotions went through my being. I wanted to hold her, let her know that everything was going to be okay and give her the life she rightfully deserved.
Unfortunately, the only thing I was able to take with me was a photograph of her.

As in a country, you never know the resources you may find in people until you get close to them. Therefore, we need to love one another and protect each other's feelings. Because in the end, whatever you do to me, you really do to yourself because I am you and you are me. We all come from one source: the Divine source.

Give a Hand

Every day you meet people with whom you do not want to associate because they are different from you. They are either from a different social circle, or economic or ethnic background. Sometimes you meet people begging you to give them a hand and you walk away without even the gratification of a little smile. You ignore them because you said to yourself why should you preoccupy yourself with others' problems.

When you needed help no one was there for you. You made a lot of sacrifices to make your dreams come true. There were days when you could not even afford a good meal. Even after trying so hard, you still encountered indifference from your employer and your family.

No one gave you a hand when you needed it. You faced all the adversities of life without the help of others. Why should you care about other people's needs or problems?

I am here to tell you that you have the power to help those people in need because you have been through hardships. You can help because you know how hard it is for people to make it on their own.

Sometimes you see beggars on a street corner and walk past them. You convince yourselves that there are governmental or social institutions designed to help them while you walk away. While it is true that there are social agencies to help them, people often need a personal touch to alleviate their sufferings. You can make a difference in someone's life by giving her/him your personal attention.

Social agencies are usually impersonal and rife with red tapes. Needy people often lack the will or stamina to deal with them. To give a hand does not necessarily mean to give money all the time to everybody you meet. The hand can be in the form of a smile, in showing a genuine interest, in expressing virtually any sign of kindness. Giving a hand to someone at the right time can be a life-changing experience for the person you help and even for you. The people you helped may reveal to you things of which even you weren't aware about yourself. They may return your act of kindness in the least expected manner of place.

Give a hand to people. Share your gifts with those less fortunate than you are. The more you share, the more abundant your life will become. For whatever you do to people and for people you really do for yourself because you reap what you sow.

Be as fair to them as you would want others to be to you. Give to everybody a fair chance whenever you can. Remember life is full of surprises. The people you help today may be the ones helping you later. There have been many instances where students have been in the position to repay former teachers who have showed fairness to them.

 Be fair because you never know where life will take you and who will be there to rescue you. And when you have been blessed with whatever your possessions may be, more is required of you. As stated in the Bible: "From everyone who has been given much, shall much be required."

Learn From Your Mistakes

We have a tendency to be too hard on ourselves and blame ourselves incessantly when we make mistakes. We always seem to forget that we are not perfect. We should do our best to avoid making mistakes. But when we make them, we should accept them as an opportunity to grow in order to move closer to fulfilling our mission here on earth.

We should try to learn from our mistakes. It is not an easy task for it requires facing our mistakes long enough to take stock of our actions and examine the fine print of every detail of our missteps. It is difficult because, sometimes, we feel ashamed and angry with ourselves for having been so careless. However, learning from our mistakes by facing them is necessary.

If we do not go through that process, we are bound to repeat the same mistakes. I have tried to avoid that process countless times but it did not work.

A Buddhist friend once told me: "Sara, life will keep on throwing the same lessons at you until you learn from them." She was so right because that is exactly what happened. After she told me that, I started examining the pattern of events in my life and realized that, for about two decades I kept repeating the same mistakes because I had not been learning from them. No matter how far ahead of the game I thought I was, I would end up at the same place. My life seemed to be going in a circle.

As a result of being inattentive to the lessons of life, I was being forced to repeat the same courses. When life teaches us lessons that we fail to understand and apply, we are forced to repeat them. The lessons of life are practical ones and have a purpose. They are to guide us throughout our journey on earth. They are not to be taken lightly.

Take every mistake as an occasion to grow and as failed quizzes before taking the final exam. Remember that all human beings often do things of which they are not proud to themselves and to others. We all make decisions we regret with consequences we wish we could reverse. Unfortunately, we cannot do that, but what we can do is to forgive ourselves and learn from our errors in order to move on with our lives.

Practice Humility

Be humble! Do not let your ego get in the way of your decency as a human being. Do not let it make you lose touch with the important things in life.

No matter how much money you have, how much you have achieved in your professional life, how much power you have and how many people you have under your command, you need to practice humility. If you don't do it willingly, the adverse

lessons of life will force you to become humble, for life is a school and we learn whether we want to or not.

Many people confound humility with weakness. Practicing humility is really a sign of strength; a sign of control or mastery over the many dance steps of life.

To have all the power and to refuse to misuse it is strength. As Shakespeare remarked: "It is excellent to have a giant's strength… But it is tyrannous to use it like a giant."

Clean Up Your Mess

No one is responsible for the messes piled up along your path but you. Therefore, it is your task to clean them by weeding out the overgrown brambles blocking your steps towards your destination.

The best way to achieve this endeavor is through daily meditation and self-introspection, which facilitate the release of the debris in your life into the universe for transformation.

The benefits of removing the stumbling blocks are identical to those of a well- kept home in which everything is easy to locate.

Being organized is also crucial to your physical and mental welfare. It allows you to reach that special place inside yourself--- your sanctuary--- in which you can make sensible decisions in accordance with the cadence of the universe.

Being organized brings peace into your life, drives out confusion and helps you start each day of your journey with a fresh outlook and renewed energy.

Learn To Negotiate

Negotiation is crucial to the survival of mankind. All human beings are unique. We each have abilities that others lack and that are fundamental to the rhythm of the Universe. That is why it is important for all of humankind to work together by sharing our gifts, talents, and experiences.

It is clear that our Creator did not intend for us to make it alone in the Universe; otherwise, He would have given everyone the same abilities.

Because we lack what others have, we are forced to team-up with one another, to learn from one another, to rejoice with one another in times of joy, to comfort one another in times of pain, and to confront the daily challenges of the Universe together in order to survive.

Watch Your Steps

Make sure you thoroughly examine whatever steps you take in life. Whatever decisions you make or predicaments you find yourself in today have the power to follow you for the rest of your life. It is true that no one is perfect. We all, at some point in our lives, may take a wrong turn.

Sometimes in life we have to get lost in order to find our way. I would like you to watch your steps in order to get to your destination with fewer obstacles and fewer delays. I suggest that you carry a map with you whenever you plan to travel afar.

By traveling afar, I mean, when you are planning to make long- term decisions such as choosing a career, getting married, and so forth. The map carried may be rules or lessons learned from your experiences.

Of course, pulling this map out whenever you have to make a decision could make life very boring. Sometimes it is fun to be a bit more spontaneous.

To carry a map and to consult it whenever you are not sure about which way to go could be the wisest thing to do. When you find yourself at a crossroad --- as we all eventually do --- it is time to pull out your map.

Learn Detachment

Do not get too attached to anyone or anything. Take whatever moment or time you spend with people you love as a gift and whatever material possessions you acquire as a bonus. Nothing and no one last forever. Whatever you have today may be gone tomorrow or at any given moment.

That is why it is important to be ready to travel solo, to let go of partners, pupils, teachers, and material possessions in order to learn new lessons, and embrace new experience.

Learn to let go because trying to hold on will only delay your learning process and your advancement in the School of Life; it will also create discord, disharmony and pain. Learn to let go and trust that if you fall, God will catch you.

Learn To Empathize

Do not criticize others' actions until you have walked a mile in their shoes. Always try to put yourself in someone else's place before you judge that person. Take time to understand another's point of view.

Remember that you are not always right and there are different ways of solving problems. Broaden your point of view because no matter how much knowledge you may have, and no matter how remote may be the feasibility of the speaker saying anything new and useful to you, it is possible that he/she may be the bearer of a message that could change your life.

Always remember that everybody is a messenger and a teacher in the School of Life.

Learn To Trust

Trust is an essential element in living a peaceful life. Trust requires taking a leap of faith because there is no guarantee that the people, we trust are worthy of our trust. But the alternative is pretty solitary.

Imagine going through life not trusting a soul and looking behind your back all the time, expecting at every moment that someone might stab you in the back. Imagine the energy wasted while doing so. That energy could have been put toward productive activities.

I know that sometimes it is hard to trust people, especially when you have been betrayed and hurt. By being vigilant, you can trust again and be protected against unworthy people.

Do not be paranoid; give everyone the benefit of the doubt unless proven unworthy of your trust.

And, if you want to have trustworthy friends, be trustworthy yourself. Remember the law of karma: what goes around comes around.

Listen to Your Intuitiveness

Listen to that little voice inside of you, which often acts like radar. Ask God for discernment to identify your inner voice from the spirit of confusion. Your inner-voice has the ability to guide you. I am not advising to rely solely upon your intuitiveness without using your objectivity or common sense.

I only want you to be aware of occurrences in this Universe that go beyond human comprehension. There have been many instances in which people have been able to resolve matters or even to save their lives just by listening to their gut feelings.

For example, many people have listened to their inner voice which told them to cancel flights, only to learn later that the planes onto which they were supposed to have boarded had crashed.

There are many circumstances in which a mechanical malfunction of a car has caused someone to return home to find out that she had forgotten to turn off the oven or the water. If those people had failed to reconsider their outings and failed to backtrack their steps, the results could have been catastrophic.

When things do not go as planned, it may be your inner voice trying to give you a message. Stand still and listen to it because that message may change or save your life. Many times, during my journey, my inner voice has guided, protected and saved me.

The most unforgettable moment occurred in March of 2000, when I was returning home from a seminar in New Orleans and got stranded at the airport for four days. I was concentrating so hard on getting out of New Orleans that I failed to pay attention to my inner voice. It took me that long to realize that the reason that I could not get out of New

Orleans was because my journey there was far from being over. I accepted the fact that it was not time to leave, and I decided to make the most of the delay and stay.

Discerning the real purpose of my being held in New Orleans was an arduous process. After an entire day of pondering, I had a revelation through a conversation with a lawyer I had met in a previous seminar who had offered me the opportunity to contribute my time and knowledge toward making one of the most valuable International Organization's annual seminar a success.

During the course of that seminar, which lasted approximately a week, I had the privilege to meet several policymakers from Latin America. The issues discussed in the workshops were directly related to my field. I had a chance to learn a number of new and sophisticated techniques that could help me advance professionally.

I also met some wonderful people in my field of expertise. Among them was a special being who turned out to be one of my guardian angels.

I believe that a Higher Force sent that being to me to uplift my spirit in a time in which I was going through some turmoil, making me doubt my ability to recoup.

I felt so squandered that I wondered if I would ever find my way back. I had just finished learning one of the most difficult lessons of life: humility. A lesson, for which, I was unprepared. As a result, my dance steps had gone out of rhythm, they were no longer in tune with the cadence of the universe.

'Stop trying to get out of New Orleans' was one of the best decisions I've ever made. That beautiful city turned out to be the classroom chosen by my guides to help me regain my sense of purpose in life. Listening to my inner voice has helped me refuel my energy and fix any broken musical strings, which needed to be in tune in order for me to go back dancing gracefully with life.

Do Not Postpone

Never postpone for tomorrow what you can do today. Live your life as if each day is the last day.

Whatever you are doing, do it well today. Why wait for tomorrow when it may never come? Or maybe the tomorrow that you are waiting for is already here since you have already had yesterday.

As stated in the Sanskrit:
> *Look well to this day*
> *For yesterday is but a dream*
> *And tomorrow only a vision*
> *But today well-lived makes every day*
> *A dream of happiness*
> *And every tomorrow a vision of hope*
> *Look well therefore to this day.*

Do Not Give Up

Every time you spin the wheel of life's fortune, it always seems to stop at the same number: the number of the eternal losers. It seems that no matter how you play the game of life, the same people always end up with its rewards.

I am here to tell you that life takes in new winners from time to time. First, you need to be sure of what you want; second, you need to be so determined and so persistent that you let nothing and no one stand in the way.

Do not let anyone stop you from achieving your goals. Do not let anything keep you from fulfilling your dreams.

Throughout life, you will meet people who will doubt your capacity for ever making it in this world. They will tell you "Do not go there, my son, my friend, my daughter, sister, my student because you will fail." They will tell you that you do not have what it takes.

Do not let your heart listen to them, when things do not go as planned. When you set goals that seem almost out of reach or almost impossible to attain, stick to them, no matter what.

Do not abandon them because of obstacles standing in your path. Only patient and persistent people obtain what they want out of life; quitters do not.

I know many talented quitters who would have made their dreams come true if only they had just one more ounce of patience. Although they were talented, they lacked one of the most important ingredients of success: "persistence."

There is this tall and strong fellow from Brooklyn, New York who recounts the times when he used to play basketball with the greatest NBA players of our time. Despite his physical strength, his height and the fact that he received the same training as his former colleagues who made it, he did not.

He lacked their mental stamina and determination. Instead of being a professional basketball player, he now lives in a basement where he manages a three-story apartment house in Park Slope where tenants give him hell when he does not fix things or clean the grass on time.

The people who made it were patient, persistent people who had faith in themselves. Even when they failed or when things did not go the way they expected, they kept on working toward their goals, their dreams; their hard work paid off.

They understood that obstacles were mere illusions, only reminders to give their best shot in whatever they were doing.

Sammy Sosa, an immigrant from the Dominican Republic, is a clear example of persistence paying off. Sosa was born to a poor family in a small town named San Pedro de Macoris. According to the Latino Legends Sports Website, in an article entitled: "A Latino Legend and A Modern Day Hero,"

Sosa could not even afford a bat, glove and ball to practice playing baseball. Instead of letting that get in the way of fulfilling his dream, he made a bat out of a tree branch, a glove out of milk cartons and a ball made of a rolled-up sock with tape around it.

Sosa overcame poverty in the Dominican Republic to become one of the greatest baseball players of our time. Sosa, a former street- vendor of orange juices and a former shoe -shiner who used to make a few cents a day, now has a multi-million Dollar contract in one of the baseball's Major

Leagues. In 1998, he was voted the National League's most valuable player; that same year; he also broke the thirty-seven-year record of Roger Maris for having been the only one to hit 61 home runs in a single season.

Sosa broke that record by hitting his 62nd home run in Wrigley Field against the Milwaukee Brewers. Sosa is still playing well as of 1999; he was the only baseball player to hit 60 home runs in two different Major League seasons.

The motivating factor behind Sosa's success as a baseball player, I suppose, was that he did not want to go back to poverty. He had a family for which to care, and he wanted to discredit the people who did not believe in him.

He had a gift that needed to be cultivated and he cultivated it to the maximum. He upheld his dream, even when he failed to perform as others expected him to do.

Many people who added their names to those of the winners in the game of life held on to their dreams. They mastered the game of life by following its rules. That is why they win all the time. Even during times of trials and tribulations, they continued working at their talent, polishing their raw diamonds until they made them shine.

As Confucius once remarked: *"The Gem cannot be polished without friction nor man perfected without trials."*

Do not even think about giving up; do not even think about walking away from your situation without a fight. Do not give up! Pull yourself together. Even if every time you take one step toward fulfilling your life's desires, you seem to two steps backward, get your spirit up and force yourself to go forward.

When you find yourself walking in one of life's dark tunnels, hold fast; continue moving forward because there will be a light at the end of the tunnel. I am living proof of that light and I testify to it

When the sky of your life seems cloudy and dark, when it seems that the climate of your life is filled with tempest and turmoil and all your dreams have been flooded, still move forward.

Good weather always comes after bad, a bright day after a dark one, and a blue sky always comes after a cloudy one.

Sosa got traded a few times to other teams because others lacked faith in his potential, but he kept working hard until he made it.

He understood that obstacles in his path were just signs to remind him to increase his energy and determination. Instead of removing himself from the path toward fulfilling his desires, he kept on going. He held on to his dreams.

A friend of mine from Lesotho, a former flight attendant, who knew how much I had been worried about my future, once sent me the following thought:
> *Hold fast to your dreams,*
> *For if dreams die*
> *Life is a broken winged bird*
> *That cannot fly.*

Never Sell Yourself Short

By selling yourself short, you cheat yourself and forfeit the well-deserved joy that you are meant to experience in life. By selling yourself short, you accept less than you rightfully deserve.

When you stoop below your level and send a message of low self-worth to your subconscious, it decreases your chance to ever regain the level of energy required to go back up.
Remember that it takes more energy to climb up than down!

Do not sell yourself short because you are worthy and unique and you deserve the best.

Your Creator loves you and believes in you. He gave you dominion over all his other creations, and only you can prevent yourself from claiming what is already yours. Stop!

Do not sell yourself short and be robbed of your birthright!

Fear Not

Living a life of fear is the worst thing that can happen to anyone. It can incapacitate your mind and your body and prevent you from performing the simplest daily chores. It can besiege your soul and your whole being throughout your life. This is a truth that I know well.

As a very young person, I was in constant fear. My existence had been filled with maybes and maybes not. Fear had crippled my mind: fear of being rejected, of not being loved, of being betrayed, of being taken advantage of, and of failure. I was so full of fear that it prevented me from sleeping at night, worrying that someone might break into the house.

In the subway, I was always worried that someone was just waiting to attack me. And one day, someone did attack me in the subway because I had created that thought-form by thinking about it all the time.

You are what you think! As the statement of Job from the Bible illustrates that saying: *"For the thing which I greatly feared has come upon me and that which I was afraid of has come unto me."* As a result, I had been unable to live as full an existence as I should.

When I am in a plane, I pray non-stop in order to make it safely to my destination. A few months ago, I flew from JFK to Oklahoma City via Saint-Louis. During the flight I had such an amazing experience; it was as if God was trying to speak to me.

You know sometimes, when you are on a plane, you do not realize how high the plane is flying, you do not even realize unless there is turbulence that you are on a plane because you can walk around, go to the bathroom, watch TV and even sleep.

That flight was very smooth; I could have slept right through it if it were not for the overwhelming thought that I was trusting with my life a pilot whom I did not even know, when I could not even trust God as much. It is like something, a little voice inside of me, was telling me how much better my life would be if I let God be my pilot. At the time when these thoughts were going most intensely through my mind, the plane went through some of the whitest, clearest clouds that I have never seen.

The white clouds were floating in the bluest sky I have ever seen, and were drenched in brilliant sunshine. It was such a solemn and unusual moment. I felt that some higher Being was trying to get in touch with me. I was frightened.

Instead of feeling calm my heart was full of fear, fear of being in touch with the Highest of the Highest and not being worthy of Him, of His attention.

I feared getting in touch with my higher self. I was so overwhelmed that I decided to continue the second leg of my trip by bus. I was so terrified that I thought that continuing by bus would prevent these types of thoughts from taking over my being. I thought that being in a bus, all I would have to do is to admire the landscapes and not think.

Little did I know about how persistent God would be and how much he wanted to help me to face the many fears in my life and to inspire trust in Him. On the bus, the people sitting right across from my seat were missionaries. How did I know? Their Bibles were visibly on their laps and they were also talking about God. One man named Michael had his Bible so close to his face while reading it that I could not help asking him whether or not he was a reverend or a pastor. He quickly replied: "Yes."

Michael interpreted my question as an opening for him to preach to me. He spent hours talking to me about God and sharing some psalms and proverbs with me. In my heart I felt that God was really talking to me.

Another event that convinced me involved a very annoying fellow on the bus, who took pleasure in getting on everyone's nerves, especially the missionaries. I found myself thinking that if I had continued traveling by plane, I would have gotten there already, if only I've had the courage to face these thoughts that were overwhelming me.

This trip made me realized that only God has the power to decide whether or not something is going to happen to you, the location and the date of its occurrence.

There is no possible escape, wherever you are, if something is meant to happen to you it will happen. And I promised myself that I should do my utmost to control my fear and enjoy my life Before that trip, I had a dream that also taught me that confronting my fears was the only way to have a healthy life:

> *My brother Marc, who had passed away in 1990, was carrying a bunch of arrows with which he took pleasure in attacking me. As he was sending them in my direction, I continued running, hoping that none of the arrows would hit me in my back. As I was running in my dream, I started questioning myself about why I was running and why would my late brother hurt me? I reasoned with myself that my late brother and I grew up together, that we were only two years apart and had often played together. Why would he hurt me? Suddenly, I stopped running and faced him. As soon as I stopped running, he put the arrows down and spoke amiably to me.*

After these two events, I resolved to try not to be as paranoid as I habitually had been and to try to control my fear. Especially when I worried about a situation that turned out better than expected. As I think about it, I realize how much energy I've wasted worrying about things that never happened, and how I could have used that wasted energy to have a more productive life.

Do not go through the same torment that I went through. Free yourself from negative thoughts that hold you down and impair your mental capacity to function as a productive human being. Have a mantra that allows you to think positively.

Have faith, even in the darkest moments of your life; convince yourself that everything is going to be okay. Convince yourself that there is nothing that can happen to you if your Creator does not allow it, and that he loves you so much that he will not let any harm come to his beautiful sons and daughters.

Have so much faith in whatever God you believe in that you leave no room for doubt or second guessing. You can create an environment where only positive things can happen to you.

Ask for Forgiveness

When you have done hurtful things to others--- whether by mischief or mistake--- recognize the errors of your ways, humble yourself and ask for forgiveness. By doing so, you may be saving yourself and the people you hurt a lot of heartache.

Do not be ashamed to put your ego on the line. With a vengeful attitude nobody wins. No matter how 'good' you might feel after getting even, you will have to answer for your misdeeds sooner or later. You will never be able to know when the betrayed party is going to retaliate. As a result, you will never have a moment of peace because you will have to keep watching your back.

The only way to get out of this vicious circle is to ask for forgiveness and hope that the other person is a big enough person to let go and strive to make things better. By asking for forgiveness, you will also help the other person move on with her life by releasing the anger or resentment that she may feel from being hurt and betrayed.

Never forget that life is a two-edge sword. If you find it difficult to ask for forgiveness, ask for guidance from your Creator through prayer.

When I have to forgive people who hurt me, or be forgiven I always find strength through prayer; I believe true forgiveness comes from a higher Being than ourselves. Let me share my prayer for forgiveness with you:

> *Lord, forgive my trespasses,*
> *For I was senseless.*
> *It never occurred to me that my missteps*
> *Were disturbing the rhythm of the Universe.*
> *Until you opened my eyes, dear Lord*
> *I failed to see that my actions were affecting others*
> *And disharmonizing the musical chords of life.*

Give me another chance, Dear Lord
Because I now understand that in order to
rid the world of its pains and discords, I
need to replace hatred with LOVE
Anger with forgiveness,
Isolation with togetherness.
Forgive me Lord and lift me up when I stumble
Lighten my path,
So, darkness can no longer
Block my view to your Kingdom.

Give Thanks

Give thanks to God regularly to acknowledge the refinement of life and cherish its gifts that have been bestowed upon us.

As written in the Bible: *"Give thanks unto the Father, which hath made us to be partakers of the inheritance of the Saints in light Who hath delivered us from the power of darkness and hath translated us into the kingdom of his dear Son in whom we have redemption through his blood, even the forgiveness of sins."*

Give thanks to people who have made a difference in your life through their smiles, generous gestures and continuous presence by your side, in times of both turmoil and celebration. Do not be indifferent to people's acts of kindness, understanding or love.

As Williams James believed*: "The deepest principle in human nature is the craving to be appreciated."*

Give thanks to people by letting them know how much they have helped you and have made a difference in your life. Give them the recognition they deserve; sometimes publicly, if doing so helps their career or advancement in any shape or form.

Give thanks to yourself --- especially to your own corporeal vessel--- for making your journey here on earth enjoyable.

How could you enjoy the beautiful vistas of life, the miracle of a sunrise and a sunset... without your eyes?

How would you be able to appreciate the beautiful melodies of the Universe through the falling of the rain, the blowing of the wind, the songs of the birds, and the waves of the ocean, and how could you dance to melodies ...without your ears?

How would you enjoy the scent of blooming flowers, the scent of the amazing blue salty sea, the smell of dirt after the rain... without your nose?

How would you be able to caress your beloved, hold the hands of a first born to guide her through her first steps, touch so many people in various ways without your hands?

How would you be able to enjoy the ecstasy of your first kiss without your mouth, and define yourself instead of leaving the task to other people without your tongue?

How would you be able to get to the diversified classrooms of life without your feet and your legs?

Give thanks to all parts of your corporeal vessel for making your life and journey on earth possible.

Do not forget your enemies while giving thanks because, believe it or not, they were used as instruments to help get out of your shell and fight for what you deserve.

This is how I usually give thanks:

I thank God for accompanying me through my journey.
I thank all the invisible forces for protecting me:
As well of the spirit of my ancestors and others.
I thank my parents for welcoming me into this world and
For guiding my steps into the diversified
Classrooms of life.
I thank my corporeal vessel
That I could never have done without.
I thank my enemies for they have been my greatest teachers.
I thank my times of celebration and turmoil
For teaching me about the duality of life
I thank the kindness of strangers
For brightening my journey with kind words, and smiles

And I thank you for welcoming
"How To Dance With Life into your life"
I hope that its principles can make
A difference in your life.

Take Notes

Your Favorite Quotes

How do you dance with life?

www.ingramcontent.com/pod-product-compliance
Lightning Source LLC
Chambersburg PA
CBHW070927010526
44110CB00056B/2253